A TASTE OF WEST AFRICA

Colin Harris

Wayland

Titles in this series

A TASTE OF

Britain	Italy
The Caribbean	Japan
China	Mexico
France	Spain
India	West Africa

Frontispiece *Young girls from Nigeria selling kola nuts.*

Cover *A village in Dogon Territory, Mali.*

Editor: Joanne Jessop
Designer: Jean Wheeler

First published in 1994 by
Wayland (Publishers) Ltd
61 Western Road, Hove
East Sussex, BN3 1JD, England

British Library Cataloguing in Publication Data
Harris, Colin
Taste of West Africa.—(Food Around the
World Series)
I. Title II. Series
641.5966

ISBN 0-7502-1205-5

Typeset by Dorchester Typesetting Group Ltd
Printed and bound by Lego, Italy

Contents

The countries of West Africa

West Africa is a vast area of Africa, stretching 3,000 km from north to south and 6,000 km from east to west. If you look at the map on page 5, you can see all the countries that make up West Africa. The Atlantic Ocean is a natural boundary to the south and west of the area. The northern boundary extends to the Sahara Desert. In the east it is more difficult to tell where West Africa ends. The people of western Cameroon say they live in West Africa, but the Adamawa highlands, between Nigeria and Cameroon, are generally accepted as the eastern boundary.

A herd of cattle in the dry savannah of West Africa.

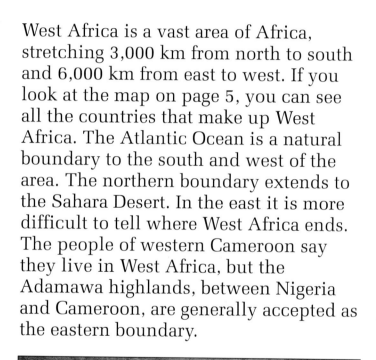

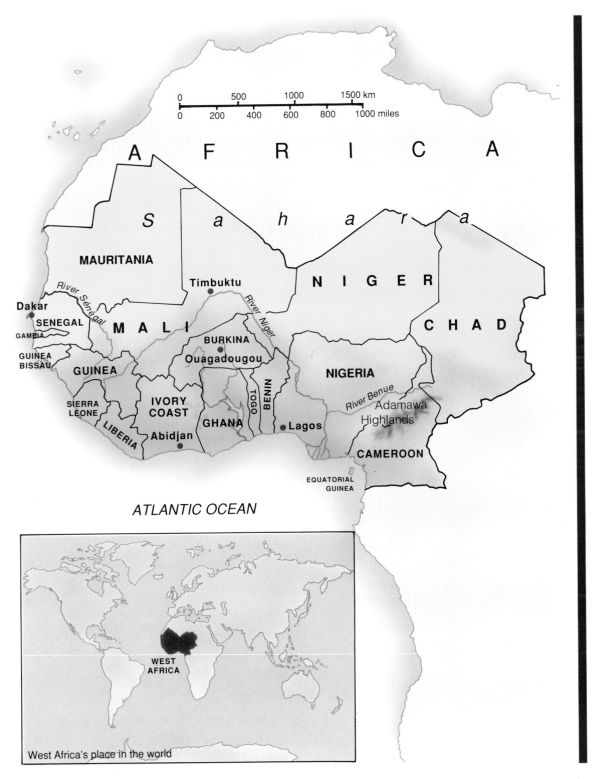

ATLANTIC OCEAN

West Africa's place in the world

A taste of West Africa

Dakar, in Senegal, is one of the many large and interesting cities in West Africa.

Most West Africans live in small villages. This village is in the southern rainforest.

Most countries of West Africa have grassland with scattered trees, called savannah. In the north, the savannah blends into dry sahel where few trees grow. But West Africa also has colourful rainforests, wide rivers, broad and shallow lakes, sandy beaches and forested mountain slopes.

West Africa has a population of about 182 million. Many people live in busy and exciting cities like Dakar and Lagos, or in romantic-sounding places like Ouagadougou and Timbuktu, but most West Africans still live in small villages.

History

Towards the end of the nineteenth century, Britain and France began to establish colonies in West Africa. At one time, every country in West Africa except Liberia was a British or French colony. Although all the former colonies are now independent countries, the

A shrine in Nigeria in honour of Oshun, an ancient goddess of the Yoruba people.

colonial powers have had a lasting influence on West Africa. They brought with them new ideas, including new foods and cooking methods, and they even drew up the national boundaries that are still used today. European missionaries introduced Christianity to many West Africans.

Before the Europeans arrived in West Africa, there were several powerful and prosperous kingdoms. For example, the kingdom of Ghana flourished from the fourth to the eleventh century, when it was conquered by the Mali kingdom. The present-day countries of Ghana and Mali took their names from these ancient kingdoms. Other important kingdoms included the Songhai, the Yoruba and the Benin kingdoms.

Early in the nineteenth century, Arabs from the Sahara Desert region began to introduce the Muslim religion to northern parts of West Africa.

Climate and vegetation

West Africa lies within the broad zone known as the tropics that circles the earth on each side of the equator. West Africa has a tropical climate. This means that, instead of summer and winter, the seasons are wet or dry. It is hot all year round, except on high mountains. However, in the West African region, there are great differences in the amount of rain that falls and the kind of vegetation that grows.

The lush rainforests of the southern areas, where there is heavy rainfall.

Imagine a journey from Abidjan in Ivory Coast to Timbuktu in Mali. You would pass through three very different landscapes. At Abidjan on the southern coast, a long wet season is followed by a short dry season. There are lush rainforests where the branches of tall trees touch like fingers. This layer of high branches is called the canopy because it forms a covering like a canopy or tent with no gaps in it. As you travel northwards the wet season becomes shorter and the dry season becomes longer. The trees begin to thin out and their branches no longer touch. Bushes and then grass grow between the trees. This is the beginning of the savannah. As you cross the savannah, trees become

In northern, drier regions there is the savannah, where very few trees grow.

9

A taste of West Africa

Timbuktu is in the sahel grasslands of Mali.

fewer in number and much shorter. They have thicker trunks to store water for use during the long dry season. By the time you have reached Timbuktu you are in the sahel, where there are very few trees and only clumps of grass. In the Sahara Desert, there is no wet season at all.

Countries like Ghana, Benin and Nigeria that stretch inland from the coast have more than one type of landscape and vegetation. Other countries, such as Mali, lie within the savannah or sahel.

Small trees are scattered across the dry sahel in the northern regions of West Africa.

Food in West Africa

Crops

In rural areas, most West Africans grow their own food on small plots of land near their village. They first clear the land of trees and bushes and then plough the soil. When the rains come they plant seeds. In dry years, there may not be enough rain for the crops, so the harvest is very poor.

This woman is watering the vegetable plot near her village in Gambia.

A taste of West Africa

In the rainforest areas of West Africa, farmers clear the land and burn some of the vegetation so they can plant crops.

These cocoyams are growing in a plot of land that has been cleared in the rainforest of south-west Cameroon.

The plot of land is used for one growing season only, then it is allowed to rest for several years. This is known as the fallow period, when the trees and bushes begin to grow again. Except in very dry seasons, this method of farming, called bush fallow, provides enough food for the people of West Africa. But as the population increases, farmers sometimes return to fallow plots too soon. If the soil has not had time to recover from the last crop, it is less fertile and cannot grow healthy crops.

In the dry sahel region, lack of water can be a problem for farmers. The main crops here are millet and groundnuts, also known as peanuts or monkey nuts. Farmers of the forest and savannah areas have less difficulty growing food because the rains are more reliable. Here the main crops are cassava, cocoyam and yams. These are all root crops, which

This young girl from Ghana is feeding maize to the chickens. Most West African farmers have a few chickens or goats.

means they grow under the ground. Farmers also grow grain crops such as maize, millet and guinea corn.

West African farmers also keep chickens and goats and grow vegetables and herbs. Women and men share the farm work, but the women usually do more work than the men.

Above *This boy has climbed a coconut tree to cut down a coconut.*

Below *Picking lemons on a plantation in Ivory Coast.*

Fruit

Root and grain crops are the staple, or main, foods in West Africa; however, the area also has a wide variety of fruits. Citrus fruits such as oranges, grapefruits and limes grow in the southern forest areas, and many people have citrus trees growing near their houses. West African oranges and grapefruits have green skins even when they are ripe. Bananas, plantains and pineapples grow wild in the forests, but they are also grown on plantations. Coconut trees grow along the coast. Boys like to climb the trees and cut down the coconuts, which they enjoy for their refreshing 'milk' and sweet nutty flesh. Pawpaws are easily grown in garden plots in most parts of West Africa. Mangoes are common in the drier areas.

Right *A pineapple plantation.*

Farmers in the savannah raise cattle for meat and milk.

Cattle

Some farmers of the sahel region keep herds of cattle to be sold for meat. Thousands of cattle are herded across vast areas of the north. They frequently cross from one country to another in search of grass during the dry season. At one time the cattle travelled 'on the hoof' to markets hundreds of kilometres away. Now they are more likely to be carried by road in lorries.

Fish

Fish are an important source of protein for West Africans. The wide Senegal, Niger and Benue rivers provide a good supply of freshwater fish. Along the coast, fishermen go out in canoes and larger boats to catch fish from the Atlantic Ocean.

Before fish can be sent to inland markets, they are preserved. Women of

These fish drying in the sun were caught off the coast of Senegal.

Above Fishing in the swamps of Nigeria.

Below These women from northern Ghana are sorting the maize harvested from the fields near their village.

the coastal regions sometimes preserve fish in the traditional way by smoking them in special ovens. But shops in the towns and cities also sell frozen fish that is either imported from outside West Africa or transported from coastal regions in boxes filled with ice or in refrigerated vans.

Storing food

In the forest regions, vegetables, root crops and grains are grown throughout most of the year, although crops grow better during the long wet season. Many foods, such as yams and maize, taste best when they are fresh, but they are also stored to be eaten later. Food storage is particularly important in drier areas, where there may be long periods when there are no fresh crops.

Farmers must be very careful how they store their food. Insects and other animals that thrive in hot weather are serious pests. They eat crops growing in the field as well as food that has been harvested and stored. Each village or family compound has a large clay storage bin raised above the ground for protection against pests. When the harvest is good, the stored food lasts until the next harvest. But if the food is used up before then, people have to buy food from the market or go without. A food shortage can cause great hardship, but fortunately it does not happen very often in West Africa.

Storing millet in a Niger village.

This woman is pounding millet using a large mortar and pestle.

Grinding millet in a village in Burkina. The building in the background is used to store grain.

Processing food

Maize, millet and guinea corn are made into flour by pounding them with pestles in large wooden mortars. The flour is quite coarse but tastes good when made into porridge and cakes. Roots such as cassava are pressed and dried then pounded to make dough-like *fufu*, a very popular dish. *Fufu* can also be made from plantain, yams and cocoyams. Wheat imported from North America and Europe is milled in factories to make flour for bread.

Foreign foods

Market stalls and shops sell foods from Europe and other parts of the world. Tinned sardines and tinned milk are particular favourites. French foods such as croissants and baguettes can be found in countries such as Togo and Senegal that were once French colonies. An English breakfast of bacon and eggs is part of the menu in big hotels in former British colonies such as Nigeria and Ghana.

Above Baguettes are popular in countries that were once French colonies.
Below This grocery stall is selling many imported items.

Village life

Above *Many West African homes have corrugated metal roofs rather than traditional thatch roofs.*

Homes

The traditional West African house was built of sun-dried bricks or mud with a thatched roof made of grass. Many homes these days, even in the villages, are made from breeze blocks and have corrugated metal roofs. Villages that are near towns may have an electricity supply, but in more isolated places homes have no electricity. In the past, villagers fetched water from a well that was shared by everyone. Today, villagers still have to fetch their own water, but

Right *Stand-pipes pump water from a village well in Gambia.*

most villages have a stand-pipe that pumps water from the well. In dry areas, there may be no village well and water must be fetched from a nearby river.

In villages throughout West Africa, women have traditionally cooked in clay pots on open wood fires or on charcoal stoves made of sheet metal. Gradually, the clay cooking pots are being replaced with aluminium pots and pans.

Food

Villagers eat the food they grow themselves, which means there is not much variety. People often eat the same thing for every meal. Any extra food is sold at the local market or, if the village is near a main road, it is sold to passing travellers. At the market, villagers can buy other types of food that are not grown locally, perhaps even imported foods such as tinned milk.

Villagers often sell their extra food to passing travellers.

A taste of West Africa

Early morning is the coolest time of day, so everyone gets up very early. A typical breakfast would be maize porridge, fruit, bread and tea. But for children who have a long way to go to school, there may be no time for much breakfast. Children take their lunches with them, or if the school is nearby they come home for lunch. Evening, when all the family is together, is the time for the main meal of the day. Food is eaten with fingers, and usually served in bowls rather than on plates.

This family in Senegal is enjoying a meal in the open air.

City life

Every West African country has large modern cities, with busy traffic-filled streets, beautiful public buildings, parks, hotels and large department stores. More and more West Africans are leaving the villages and moving to the towns and cities in search of work. In Nigeria and Cameroon, there will soon be more people living in towns than in villages. City life can be exciting; there are markets, entertainment and new people

The city of Lagos is on the coast of Nigeria.

23

to meet. But many who arrive in the city cannot find jobs, so they have to move in with relatives, even distant relatives such as cousins, and rely on them to help them survive in the city.

Homes

Every city and town has large blocks of flats and solid concrete houses. These homes have running water and electricity. Food is cooked on electric stoves or bottled-gas cookers.

But many people cannot afford such luxuries and have to live in smaller, less comfortable houses. Often these houses have no running water, and neighbours have to share stand-pipes in the street.

Food

People living in towns and cities generally eat the same types of food as the villagers, but there is a greater selection of food to choose from in the markets and shops. Open-air

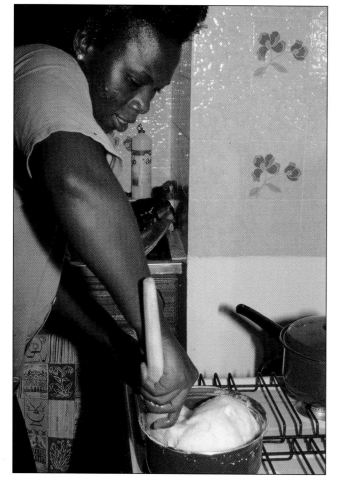

This woman is preparing banku, *a dish made with cassava and maize. Many people in the towns and cities of West Africa have gas or electric stoves, but they still follow the traditional recipes and methods of cooking.*

markets sell a wide variety of fresh fruit, vegetables, grains, meat and fish. In the cities and large towns, there is plenty of imported and frozen foods for sale at supermarkets and 'cold stores'. A cold store is a shop with a frozen food section – containing either imported or locally produced frozen food.

Eating out is not a problem in towns and cities. Street traders sell bread, roasted groundnuts, fresh sliced fruit and delicious cooked snacks. There are plenty of small restaurants known as 'chop bars' that offer cooked meals, snacks and drinks.

Supermarkets sell lots of imported foods.

West African dishes

Above Cassava, a root vegetable, is used in many West African dishes.

Below Crushed cassava being rolled into small balls.

Starchy root vegetables like cassava or yam are part of most West African dishes. The vegetables are usually boiled and served with meat or fish. Boiled yam is delicious when served with fish fried in oil and ginger. Mashed cooked yams are sometimes mixed with eggs and fried as yam balls. These are eaten plain or mixed with slices of tomatoes and sweet red peppers.

Almost every West African home has a *fufu* pounder, which is like a large mortar and pestle. Pieces of cooked yam, cassava, cocoyam or plantain are crushed in the mortar and then pounded with water until a soft lump of *fufu* is formed. The pounding is usually done outside the house. *Fufu* and pepper soup is a typical meal. Pieces of *fufu* are broken off and eaten with the fingers.

Chicken is a favourite meat in stews and soups. Locally grown vegetables and herbs may be added for extra flavour. Groundnut stew, made with chicken, crushed groundnuts, tomatoes, onions and peppers, is very popular. So is the much hotter pepper chicken stew. These dishes are served with boiled rice, yam, sweet potato or plantain.

A rich oily stew made from palm oil is a good source of vitamin B. The palm oil produces a thick orange-coloured layer on top of the stew.

Rice, which grows only in the wetter regions, is rather expensive to buy, so it is usually saved for special occasions. One party dish that is popular throughout West Africa is *Jollof* rice.

West Indian cooking

Many West African dishes are also enjoyed in the West Indies. For well over a hundred years, West African slaves were taken to the West Indies, where their recipes and their cooking traditions were passed on.

Left Palm oil for sale at a market in Togo.

Below Oil palm fruit.

A taste of West Africa

This spicy Jollof *rice and fish dish is often served on special occasions and at celebrations.*

This is a mixture of rice, tomatoes, onions, pepper and spices boiled together and served with a choice of fried chicken, beef or goat. This recipe comes from Senegal where it is the national dish of the Wolof people.

Kiliwili is a popular snack, often sold at the roadside. Pieces of plantain are coated with cayenne pepper and fried in oil. It is very hot!

West Africans eat very few cooked desserts. A choice of juicy fresh fruit is usually eaten after the main course. A favourite treat for children is to chew on a piece of sugar cane, which grows in the forest area of West Africa. Because the sugar cane is raw, it does not harm their teeth.

To be fit and healthy, West African children, like children everywhere, need a balanced diet that includes a variety of energy foods, proteins, vitamins and minerals. Children are taught at school what foods to eat in order to get elements from each of these food groups.

Most West Africans eat a balanced diet. Unfortunately, some people, especially in the drier northern regions, do not always get enough of certain foods and, therefore, may be undernourished. But this rarely happens in the south where fresh fruits and vegetables are plentiful throughout the year.

Above *In most southern countries of West Africa, fresh fruits and vegetables are always available. This girl is selling mangoes in Burkina.*

Left *This man and woman are preparing* garri, *which is pounded cassava fried in palm oil.*

Feasts

Religious festivals, weddings, funerals and special events are times for feasts. One particularly exciting and colourful celebration is the 'enstoolment' of a new chief. The chief's stool, or throne, is a specially carved seat on which he is proclaimed ruler of the people. His queen's stool is similar but slightly smaller. On these occasions, the chief and other village elders wear traditional clothes and there is drumming, dancing and feasting.

West Africans enjoy lots of different celebrations and festivals that include music, dancing and special food.

For Christians, Christmas and Easter are also times for feasts. The Muslims of West Africa celebrate the end of Ramadan – the month of daytime fasting and prayer – with a special feast.

A typical festive meal is *Jollof* rice and goat meat. Usually the grown-ups drink palm wine. This is made from the sap of certain palm trees. When the palm wine is fresh and sweet, children are allowed to drink it. But after a few days the wine becomes too strong for children.

In some parts of the south, there is a yam festival when the yams are ready to be harvested. This is a good time to have a party and enjoy a feast of fresh yams.

These dancers at a festival in Mali are wearing traditional costumes and masks.

Porridge

Ingredients

Serves 4

200 g millet
400 g water
salt
sugar

Equipment

saucepan
wooden spoon
small serving
    bowls

This porridge is made from millet and does not taste like oatmeal porridge.

Harvested millet tied in bundles.

1 Put the water in the saucepan with a little salt and bring to the boil. Add the millet.

Always be careful with boiling liquid. Ask an adult to help you.

2 Cook until soft, stirring all the time.

3 Serve in bowls and sprinkle with sugar.

Fruit salad

Fruit for sale in Abidjan, Ivory Coast.

Ingredients
Serves 6–8

1/2 pineapple
1 pawpaw
1 mango
2 bananas
1/2 coconut or
    shredded
    coconut
2 oranges
2 tablespoons
    lemon juice
1 lime cut into
    wedges

Equipment

knife
chopping board
large mixing bowl
wooden spoon
serving bowls

1 Peel the fruits and cut them in slices. Cut the pineapple into rings or wedges.

Always be careful when using a knife. Ask an adult to help you.

2 Mix all the fruit together with the lemon juice in a large bowl. Serve in smaller bowls with a wedge of lime to squeeze over the salad.

33

Kiliwili

Ingredients
Serves 4–6

2 plantains or
   unripe
   bananas
1 tablespoon
   cayenne
   pepper or
   paprika
2–3 tablespoons
   groundnut or
   corn oil

Equipment

knife
chopping board
bowl for
   cayenne or
   paprika
frying pan
tongs or fish
   slice
paper towel

Plantains are used to make kiliwili.

1 Peel the plantains or bananas and cut them into small, bite-sized pieces.

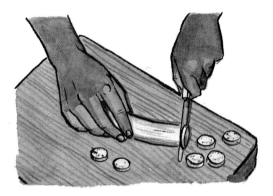

3 Heat the oil in the frying pan and fry the plantain or banana pieces slowly until they are brown and crispy on the outside.

2 Dip the pieces gently in cayenne pepper or paprika. Shake off any loose cayenne pepper. It can be very hot!

Always be careful when frying. Ask an adult to help you.

Take great care when using cayenne pepper because it can irritate your skin, mouth, eyes or any part of the body it touches.

4 Remove the pieces from the frying pan with tongs or a fish slice and drain on pieces of paper towel.

5 Serve while still warm.

Groundnut stew

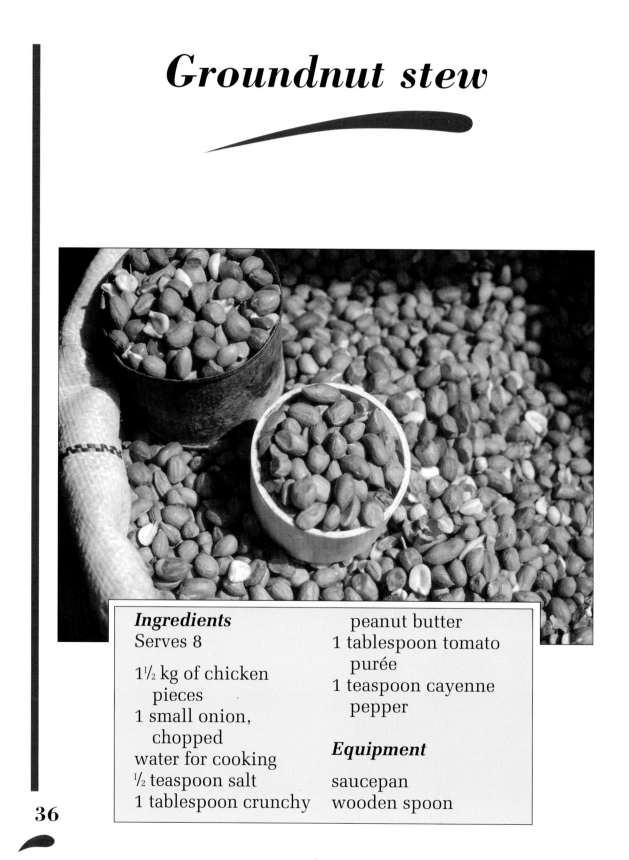

Ingredients
Serves 8

1½ kg of chicken
  pieces
1 small onion,
  chopped
water for cooking
½ teaspoon salt
1 tablespoon crunchy

peanut butter
1 tablespoon tomato
  purée
1 teaspoon cayenne
  pepper

Equipment

saucepan
wooden spoon

Always be careful with boiling liquid. Ask an adult to help you.

1 Put the chicken pieces, salt and onion in the saucepan and cover with water. Cook for about 30 minutes.

2 Add more water if necessary to cover the chicken.

3 Add the tomato purée and cayenne pepper and stir. Cook for 20 minutes.

4 Add the peanut butter and stir. Simmer for 10 minutes.

5 Serve with fluffy white rice or yam, and boiled plantain.

Fufu

Ingredients
Serves 4

2 yams,
  plantains or
  unripe
  bananas
water for boiling
hot water as
  needed for
  mixing

Equipment

saucepan
large mortar and
  pestle
serving bowls

This woman is making fufu.

1 Peel the yams, plantains or unripe bananas and cut into pieces. Boil in water until soft.

Always be careful with boiling liquid. Ask an adult to help you.

2 Put the pieces into the mortar one by one and pound carefully.

3 Add small amounts of hot water as needed to keep the mixture moist. Keep pounding and adding water until the *fufu* sticks together in one lump.

4 Divide the *fufu* into small balls and place in the serving bowls. Serve with soup or vegetables.

Jollof *rice*

Planting seedlings in a rice field in Sierra Leone. Rice is grown only in the wetter areas, but it is eaten throughout West Africa.

1 Put the rice and water into the saucepan and bring to the boil. Turn the heat down and simmer.

Always be careful with boiling liquid. Ask an adult to help you.

2 When the rice is partly cooked, mix in the tomato purée, onions, cayenne pepper, mixed herbs, thyme, butter, black and white pepper and salt.

3 Continue to simmer. When the rice is almost cooked, add the tomatoes.

4 When the rice is cooked, add pieces of fried or stewed chicken and mix together. Serve in a large bowl.

Ingredients
Serves 6–8

450 g white rice
1–1¼ l water
125 g tomato purée
1 large onion, sliced
1 teaspoon cayenne
   pepper
1 tablespoon mixed
   herbs
sprig of thyme
75 g butter
black and white
   pepper to taste
salt to taste
2 large tomatoes,
   peeled and sliced
500 g fried or stewed
   chicken, cut into
   pieces

Equipment

large saucepan
knife
chopping board
wooden spoon
serving bowl

Ginger fried fish

Ingredients
Serves 4

1 kg of rock eel
(or any firm
white fish,
such as
haddock)
½ tablespoon
ground ginger
1 onion, finely
chopped
½ teaspoon
cayenne
pepper
salt to taste
2 tablespoons
groundnut or
corn oil
parsley sprigs

Equipment

large bowl
knife
chopping board
frying pan
fish slice

A fish catch on the coast of Gambia.

Ginger fried fish

1 Cut the fish into small pieces.

3 Fry the fish in oil. Turn to fry on all sides.

2 Place in a bowl with ground ginger, onion, cayenne pepper and salt. Let stand for 15 minutes.

4 Serve with sprigs of parsley. This dish goes well with boiled yam or rice.

Pawpaw and lime

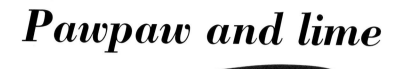

Ingredients
Serves 4

1 pawpaw
1 lime

Equipment

knife
cutting board
serving bowls

1 Cut the pawpaw into four wedges and scoop out the black seeds.

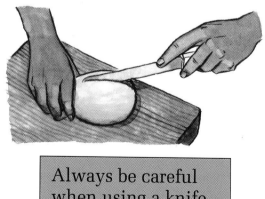

Always be careful when using a knife. Ask an adult to help you.

2 Serve each wedge in a bowl with a slice of lime on top.

3 Squeeze the lime onto the pawpaw just before eating.

Glossary

Breeze blocks Lightweight building blocks made from cinders (breeze) mixed with sand and cement.

Cassava A root vegetable, shaped like a carrot, with brown skin and white flesh.

Christian A follower of Christianity – the religion based on the teachings of Jesus Christ.

Citrus fruit A type of slightly acid fruit covered with thick skin that grows on trees or shrubs in tropical climates. Oranges, lemons, limes and grapefruits are all citrus fruits.

Cocoyam A root vegetable. A cocoyam is smaller than a yam and looks a bit like a cassava.

Colony A region that is ruled by people from another country, often referred to as the mother country.

Compound A group of houses in an enclosed space with a shared front yard and garden. A large, extended family of mother, father, children, aunts, uncles, grandparents and cousins may live together in one family compound.

Corrugated Formed into folds and grooves.

Diet The type of food a person normally eats.

Equator An imaginary line that circles the middle of the earth.

Fallow When referring to land, fallow means leaving it unused for one or more growing seasons, in order to make the soil more fertile.

Fertile When referring to soil, fertile means very rich and nourishing, thus encouraging plant growth.

Grassland Land where grass is the main form of plant life.

Groundnut (peanut, monkey nut) A type of underground bean, with two kernels that grow in a pod or shell.

Guinea corn A type of grain similar to millet that is used to make porridge or is ground into flour.

Harvest The fruit, vegetables or grains that are picked at the end of the growing season.

Imported Brought into the country from another country.

Isolated Far from any other village or town.

Millet A pale yellow grain that grows well in dry climates.

Minerals Substances such as iron and zinc that are found in certain foods in small amounts and are necessary for a healthy diet.

Missionaries People sent by a religious organization (usually the Christian Church) to a foreign country to work with people there and to teach their religion.

Mortar A very hard bowl in which substances are ground or pounded with a pestle.

Muslim A follower of the religion called Islam and the teachings of the Prophet Mohammed.

Nutrition The nourishment you get from the food you eat.

Pestle A club-shaped tool used to pound or grind substances in a mortar.

Plantain A tropical fruit similar to a banana. Plantains are treated as vegetables rather than fruit and are fried, baked or dried and ground into flour.

Plantation A large area of land used to grow a single crop, such as pineapples.

Processing When referring to food, processing means treating in such a way that the food lasts longer or can be used more easily.

Protein The main body-building substance found in certain foods.

Ramadan A month when Muslims say extra prayers, give money to the poor, and fast during the day.

Rural Of the countryside.

Sahel A region of dry savannah south of the Sahara Desert.

Savannah Grassland with few trees.

Traditional According to tradition, which is a way of doing something that has not changed for years.

Tropical Having to do with the tropics, the area around the equator that is hot all year round.

Undernourished Not receiving all the vitamins, minerals and proteins needed to stay healthy.

Vitamins Substances found in foods in tiny amounts. Vitamins are necessary for normal growth and general health.

Yam A root vegetable with brownish-pink skin and white flesh.

Further information

Africa by Keith Lye (Franklin Watts, 1987)

African Food and Drink by Martin Gibrill (Wayland, 1989)

Food around the World by Ridgwell and Ridgeway (Oxford University Press, 1986)

Nigeria by Kamala Achu (Wayland, 1993)

Peoples and Nations of Africa by Sheila Fairfield (Young Library, 1987)

Picture acknowledgements

The publishers would like to thank the following for allowing their photographs to be reproduced: Anthony Blake Photo Library 44 (K. Kleineman); Chapel Studios: Zul cover inset, 20 top (Nicola Swainson); Christine Osborne Pictures 9, 20 bottom, 21, 25, 26 bottom, 28, 36; Eye Ubiquitous 6 top, 27 left (Thelma Sanders), 34 (Trip), 42; Panos Pictures, 10 top (David Reed), 11 (Trygve Bolstad), 14 top (Penny Tweedie), 14 bottom left and right (Ron Giling), 15 both (Jeremy Hartley), 16 both (Bruce Paton), 17 (Ron Giling), 18 bottom (Jeremy Hartley), 19 top (Ron Giling), 22 (Jeremy Hartley), 29 top (Ron Giling), 32 (Rex Parry), 33 (Ron Giling), 40 (Jeremy Hartley); Edward Parker 4, 6 bottom, 10 bottom, 12 bottom, 12 top (P. E. Parker), 27 right (P. E. Parker), 31; Tony Stone Worldwide cover; Tropix 13 (M. & V. Birley), 19 bottom (M. & V. Birley), 24 (M. & V. Birley), 26 top (D. Parker), 38 (M. & V. Birley); Wayland Picture Library *frontispiece,* 7, 8, 23, 29 bottom, 30 (all by James Morris).

The map artwork on page 5 was supplied by Peter Bull. The recipe artwork on pages 32 to 44 was supplied by Judy Stevens.

Index